Learning Takes Patience

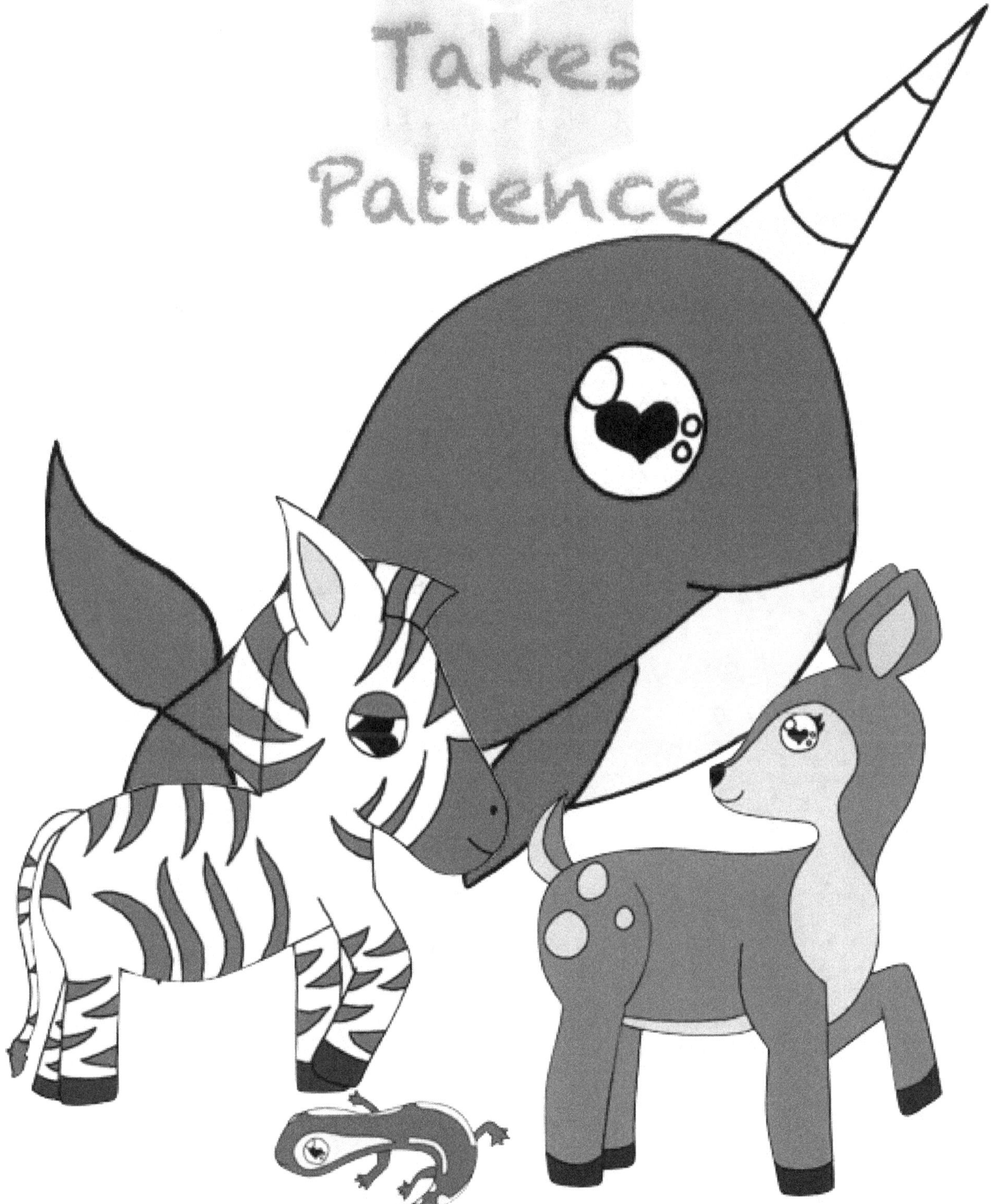

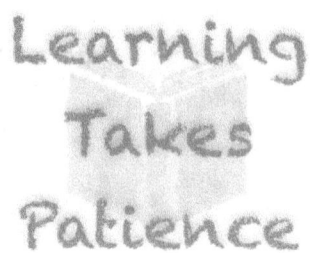

Learning Takes Patience

Patience K & Mary C Warren

First printing: January 2020

Copyright © 2020 by Patience K & Mary C Warren. All rights reserved. No part of this book may be used or reproduced in any manner whatsoever without written permission of the author.
ISBN: 9781661767778
Imprint: Independently published

For information write:

        Learning Takes Patience
        16258 Hailey Lane
        Saint Robert, MO 65584

Aa
For Alligator

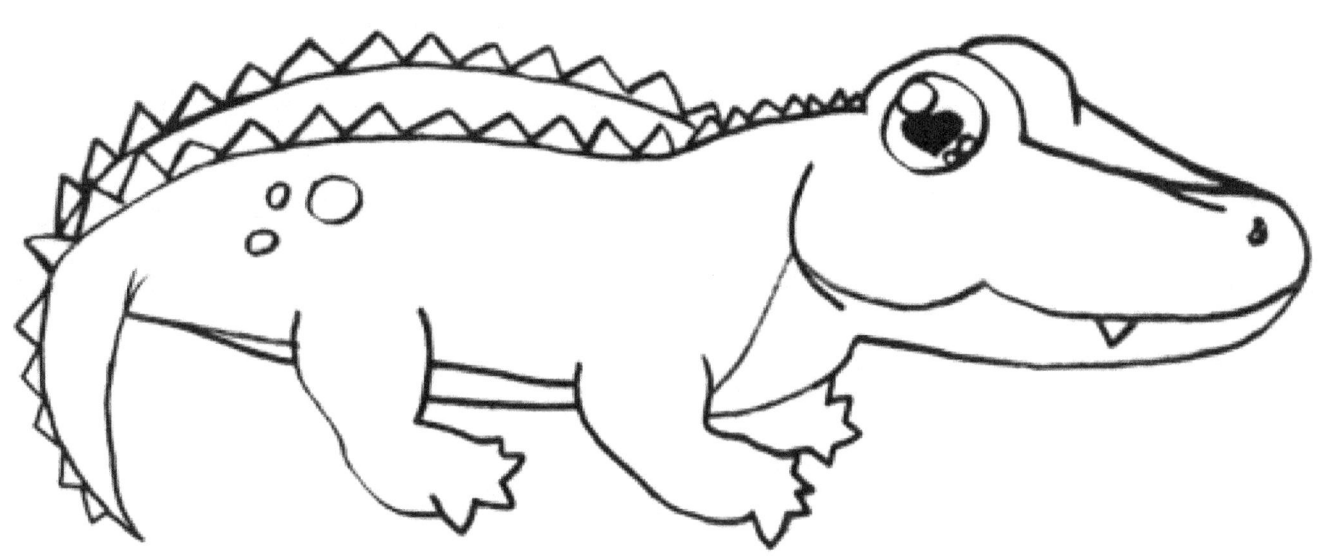

Name_____

Learning Takes Patience

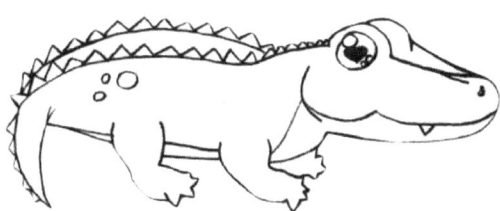   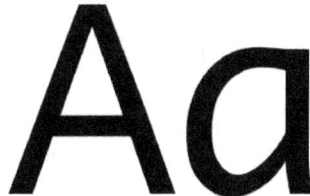

Bb
For Bat

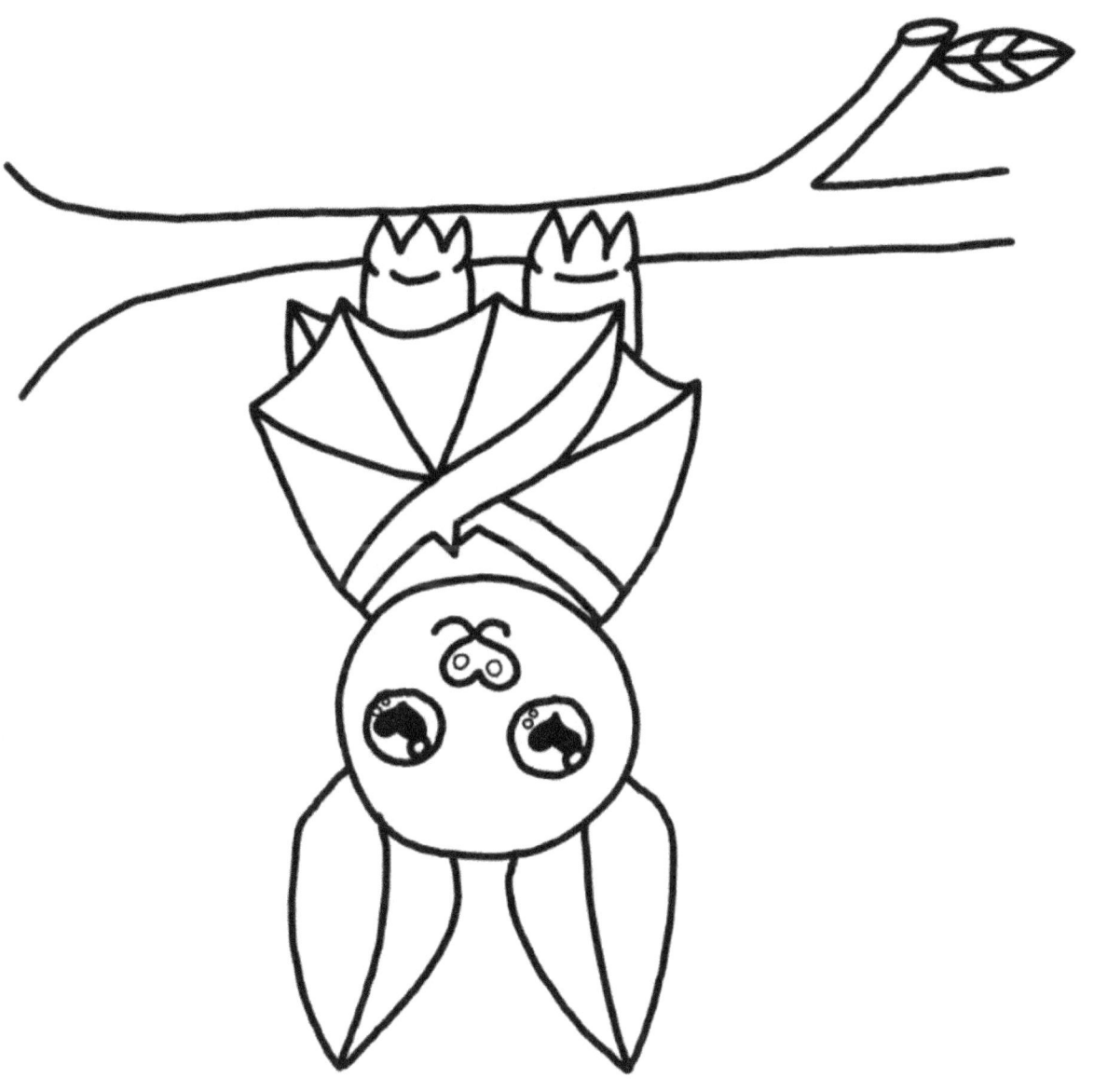

Name_____

Learning Takes Patience

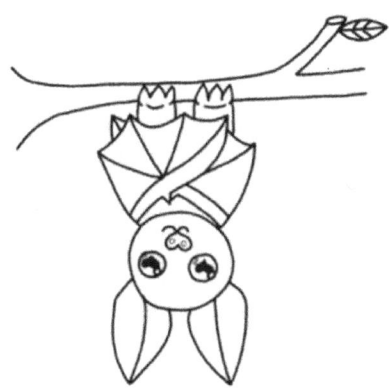

Bb

Cc
For Cow

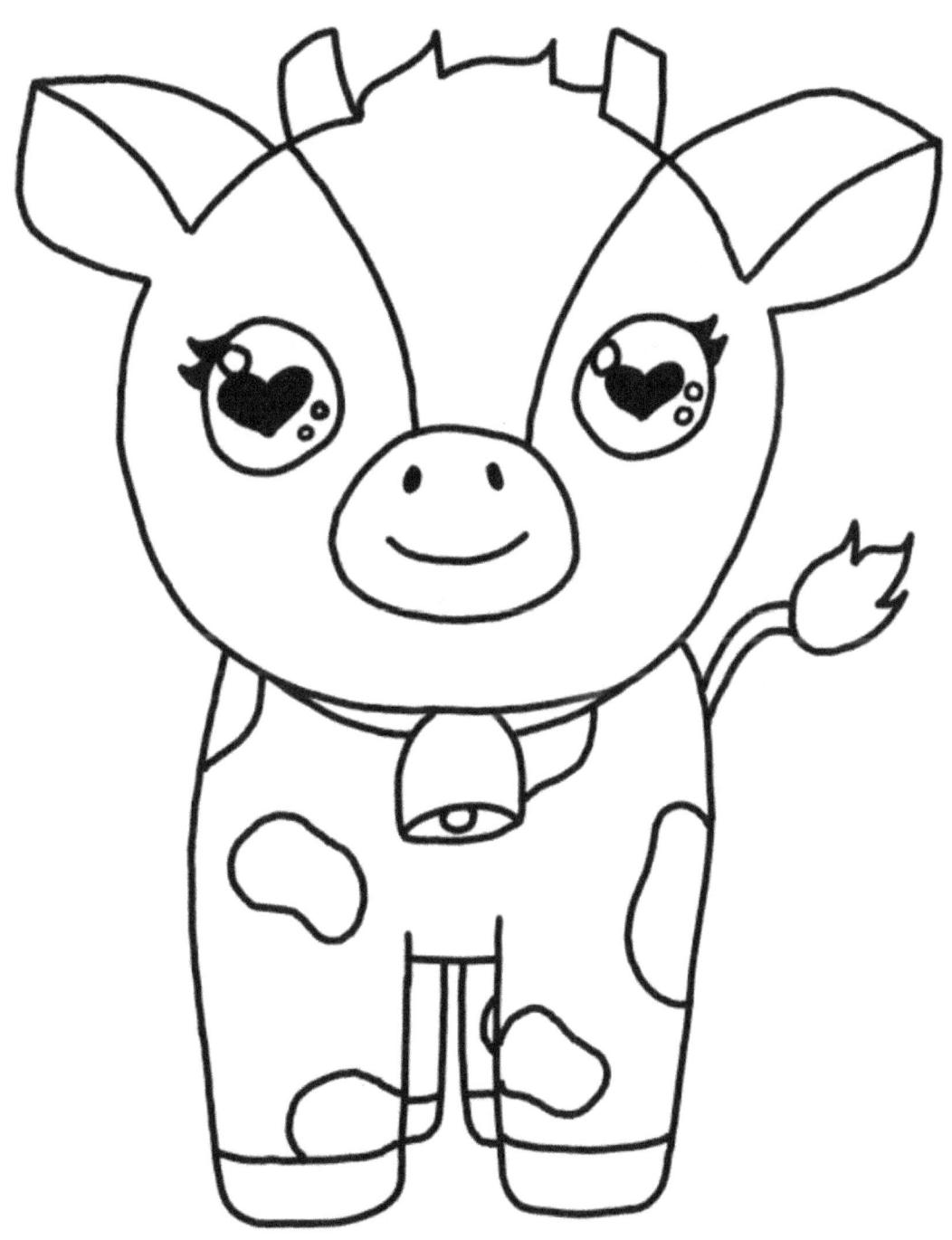

Name_____

Learning Takes Patience

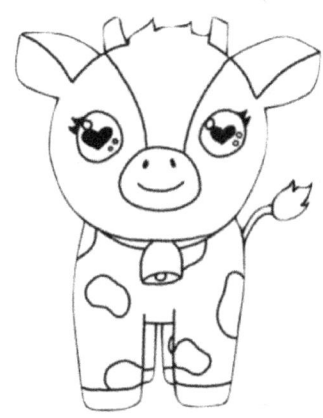

Cc

_____
- - - - - - - - - - - - - - - -
_____
- - - - - - - - - - - - - - - -
_____
- - - - - - - - - - - - - - - -
_____
- - - - - - - - - - - - - - - -
_____

Dd

For Deer

Name_____

Learning Takes Patience

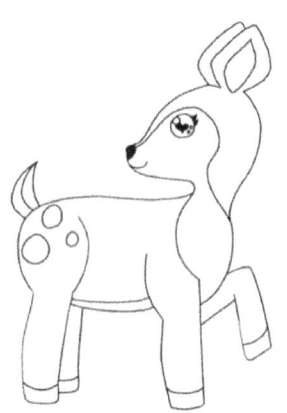

Dd

_____
- -
_____
- -
_____
- -
_____
- -
_____

Ee
For Elephant

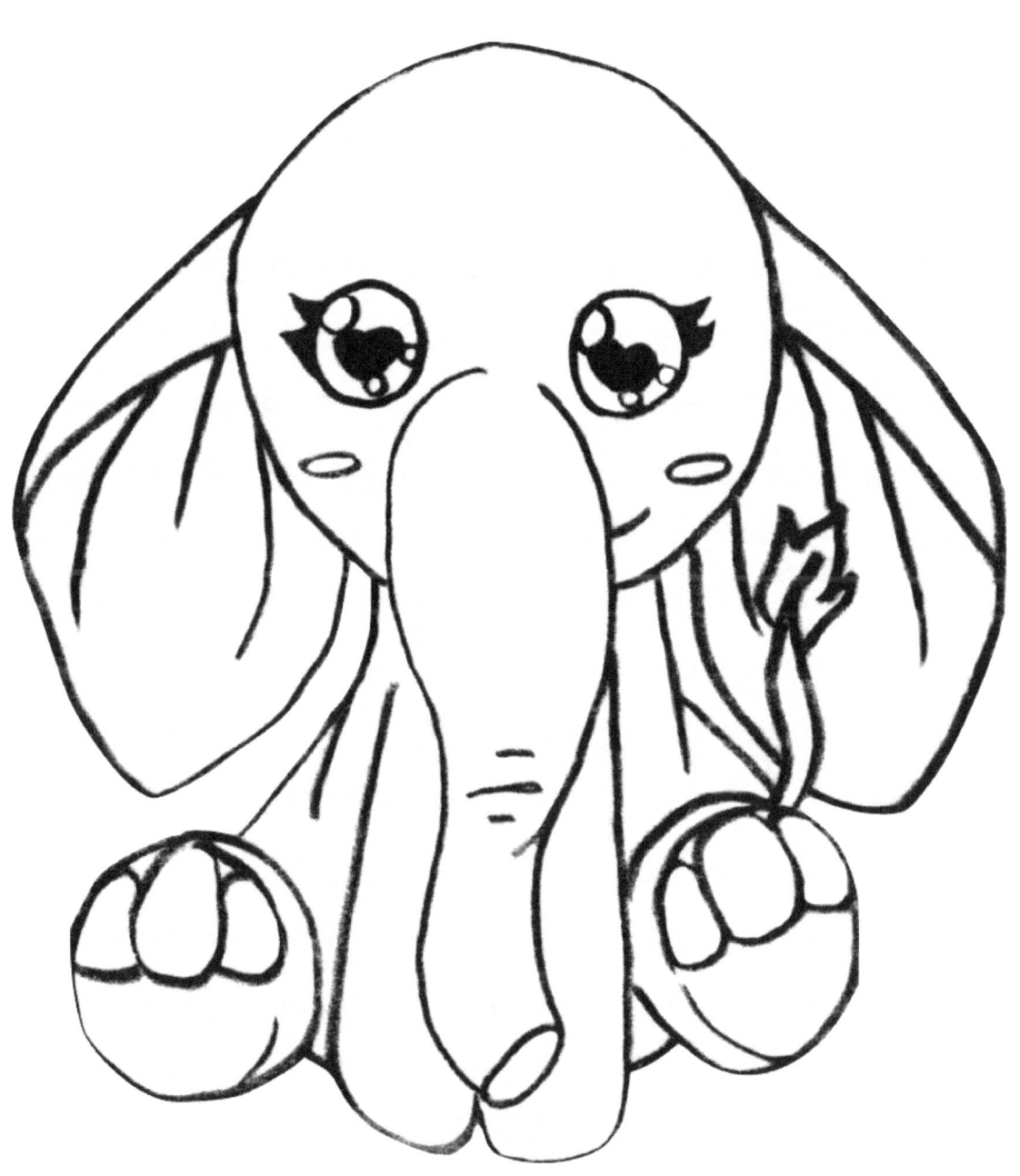

Name_____

Learning Takes Patience

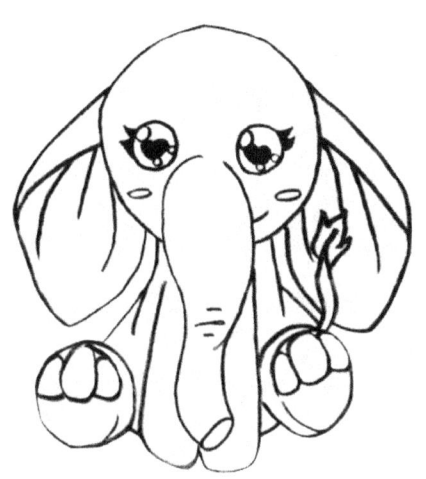

Ee

Ff
For Fox

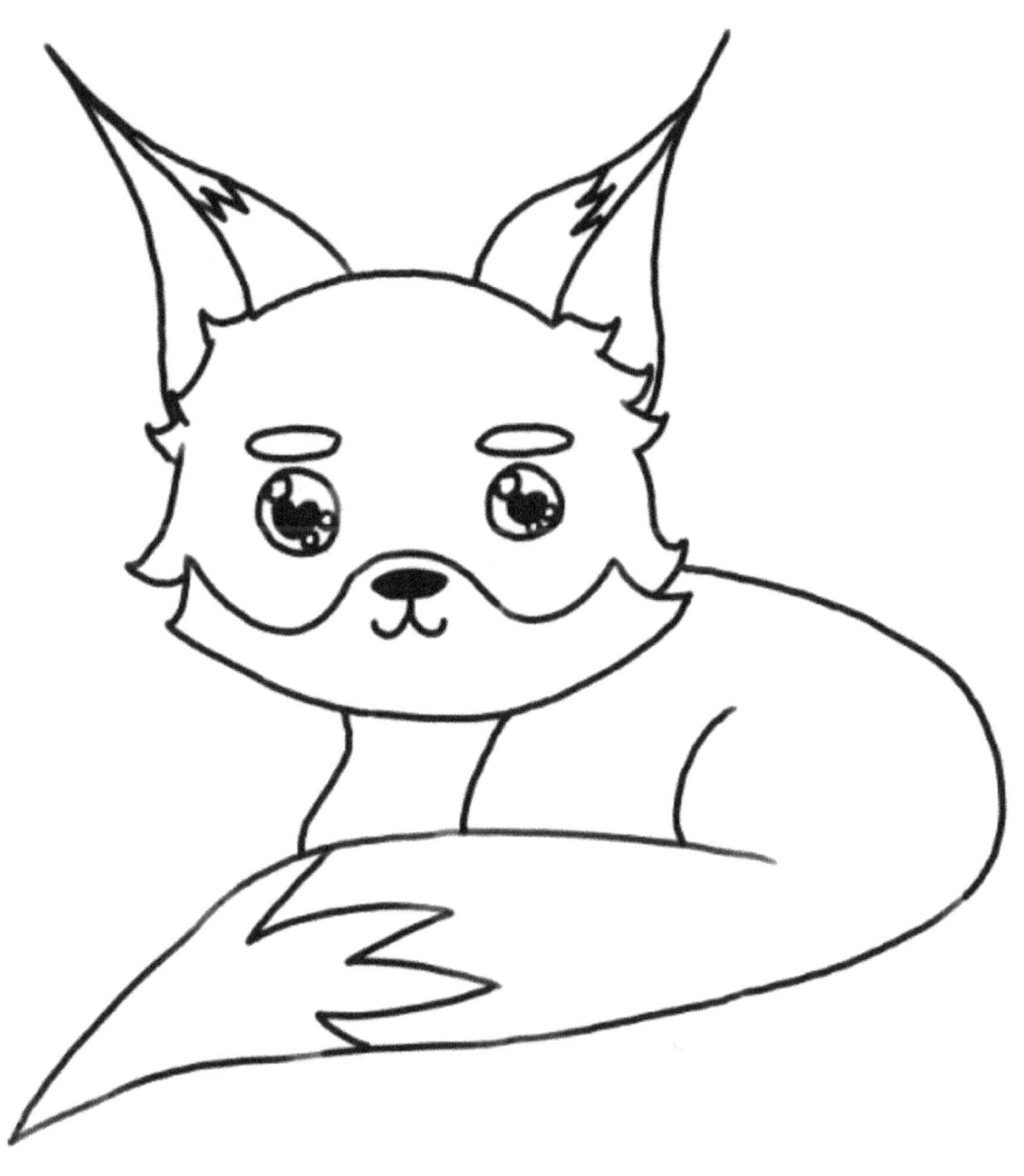

Name_____

Learning Takes Patience

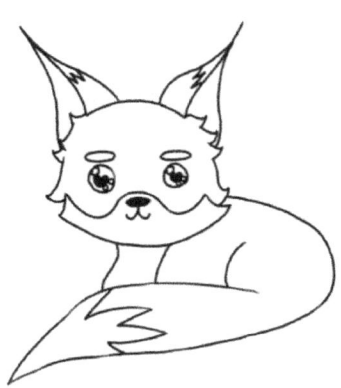

Ff

Gg
For Giraffe

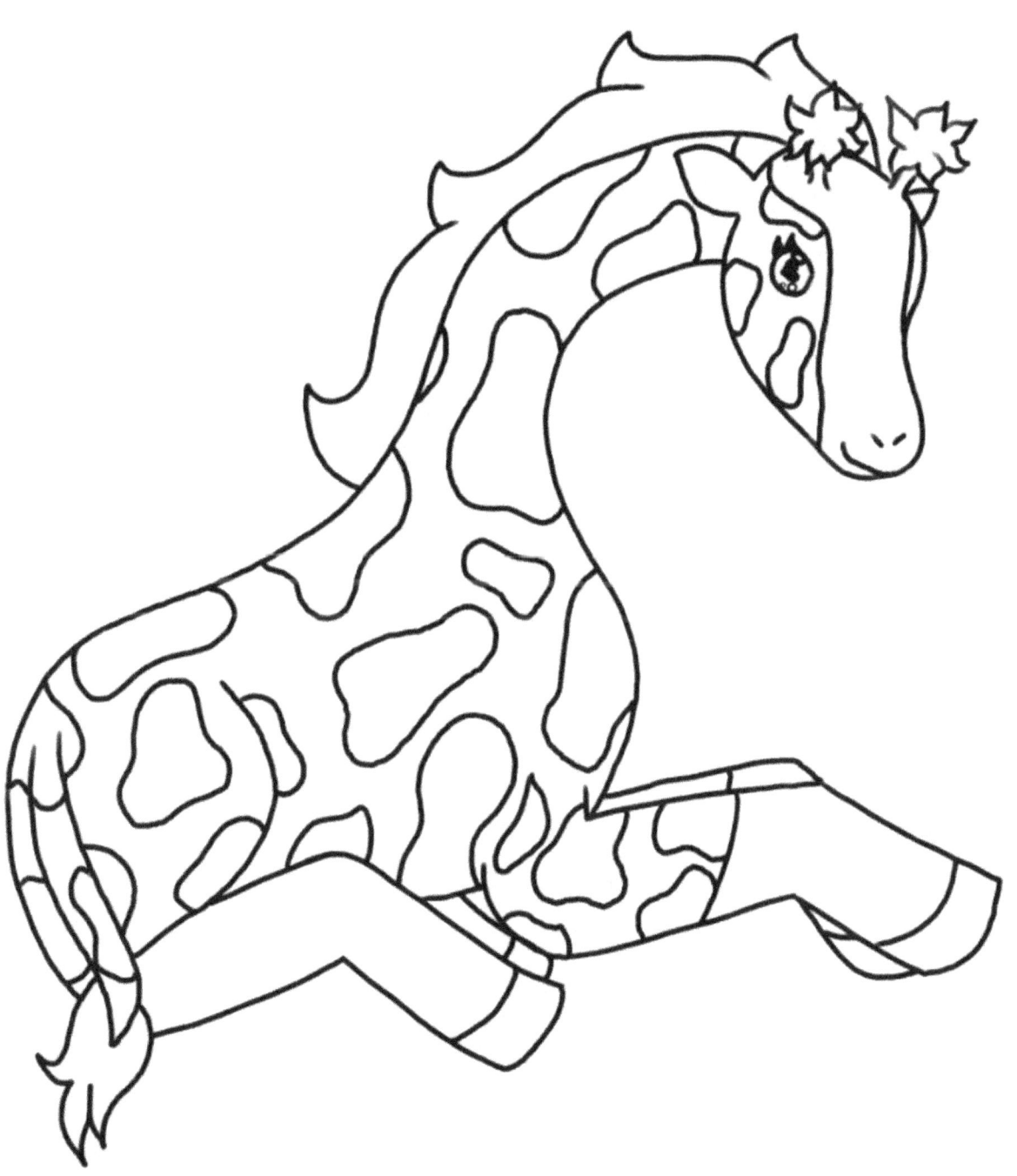

Name_____

Learning Takes Patience

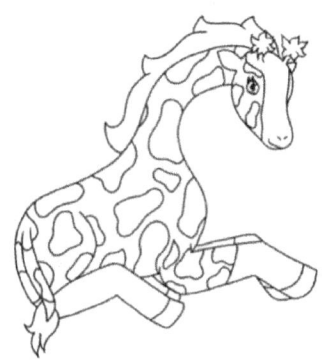

Gg

Hh
For Hedgehog

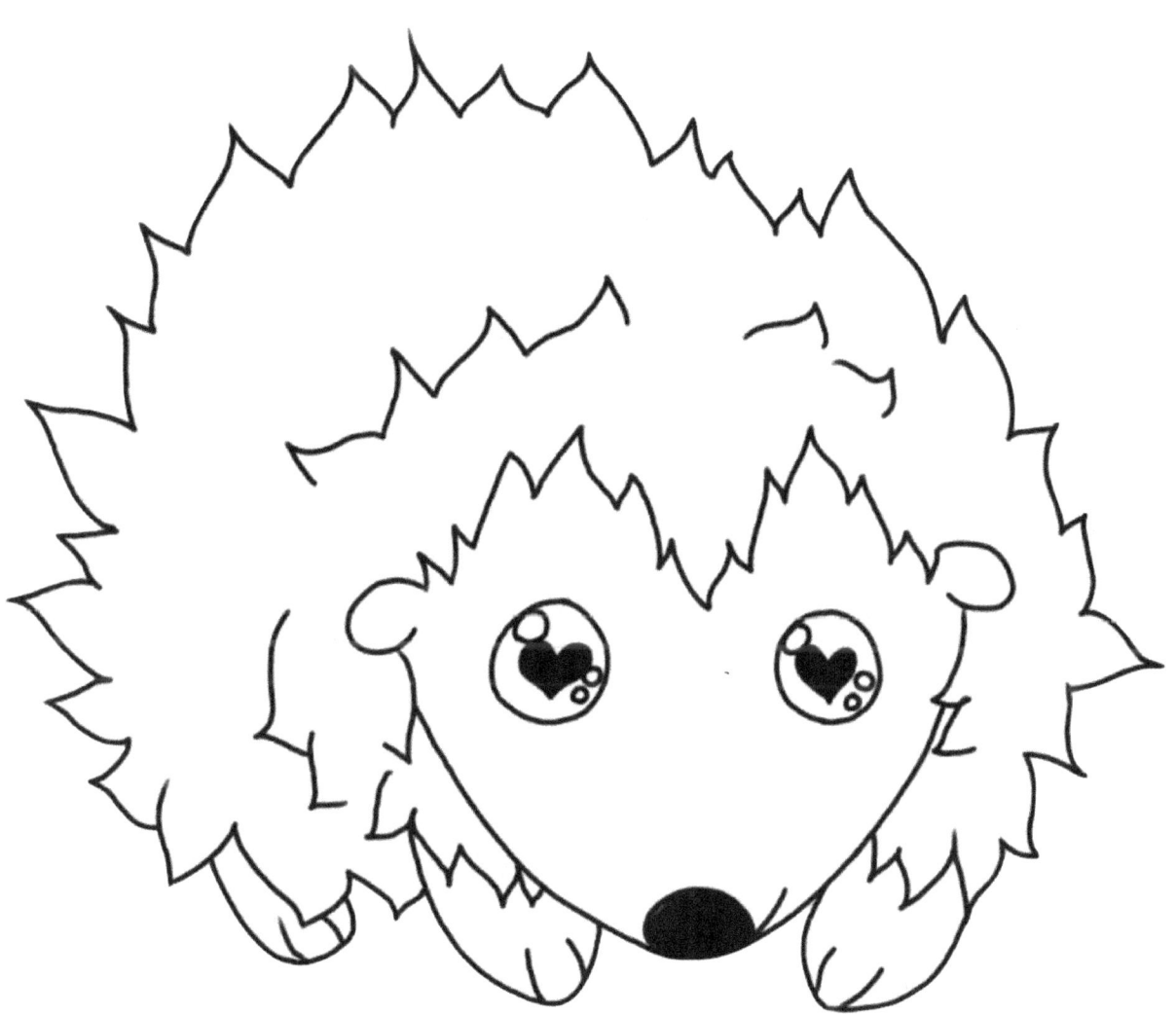

Name_____

Learning Takes Patience

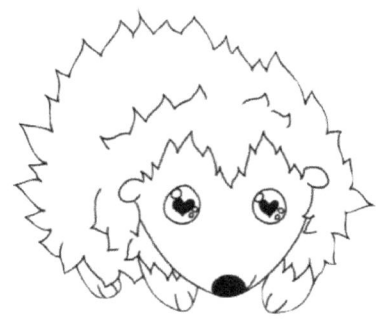

Hh

_____
- - - - - - - - - - - - - - - - - -
_____
- - - - - - - - - - - - - - - - - -
_____
- - - - - - - - - - - - - - - - - -
_____
- - - - - - - - - - - - - - - - - -
_____

Ii
For Ibis

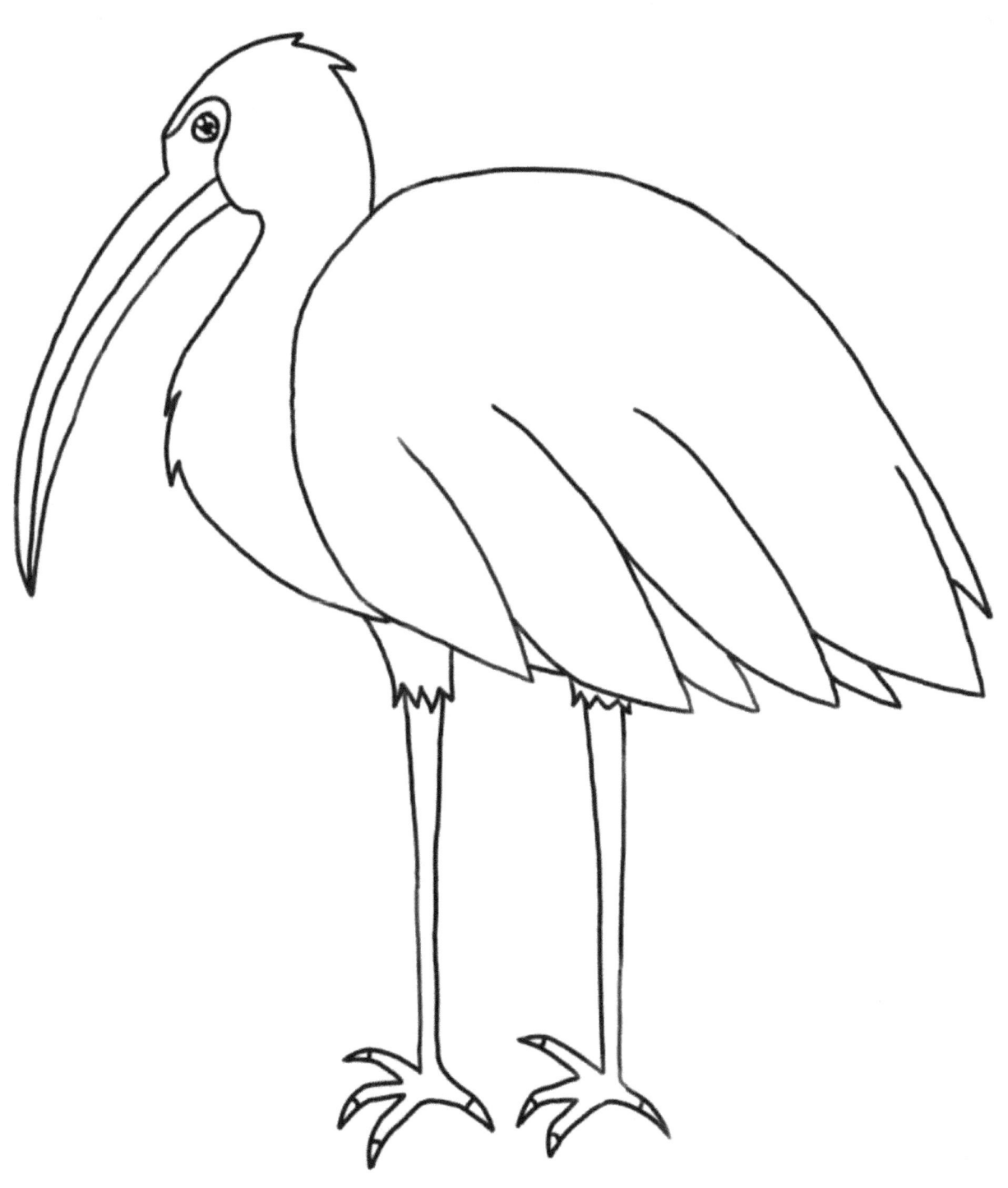

Name_____

Learning Takes Patience

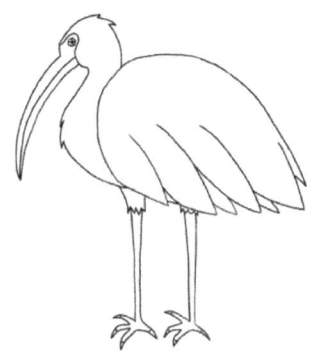

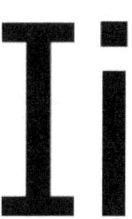

Jj
For Jellyfish

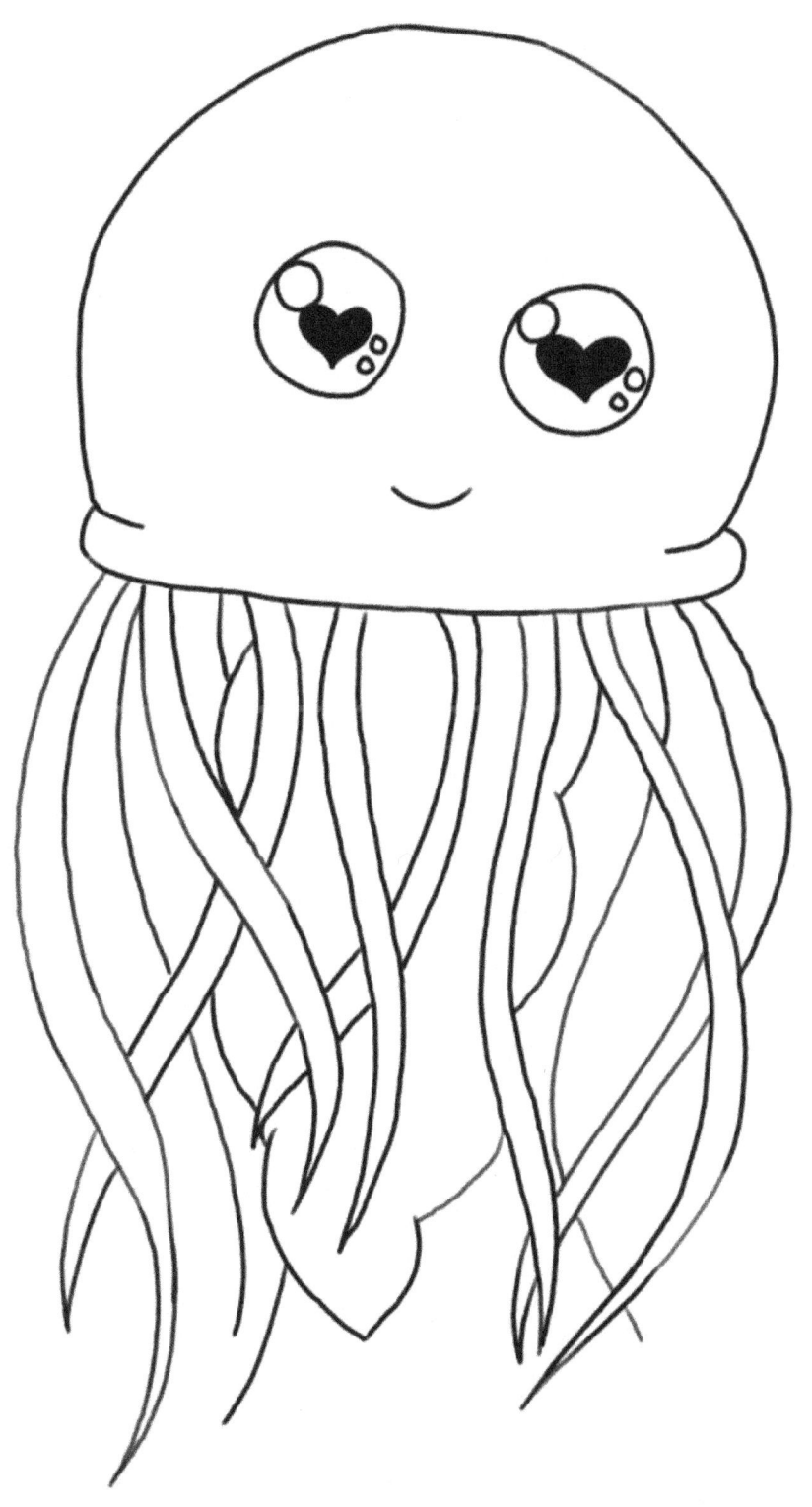

Name_____

Learning Takes Patience

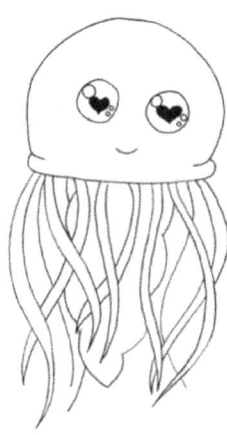

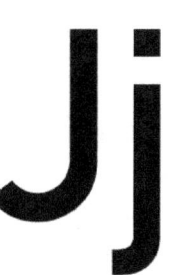

Kk
For Kiwi

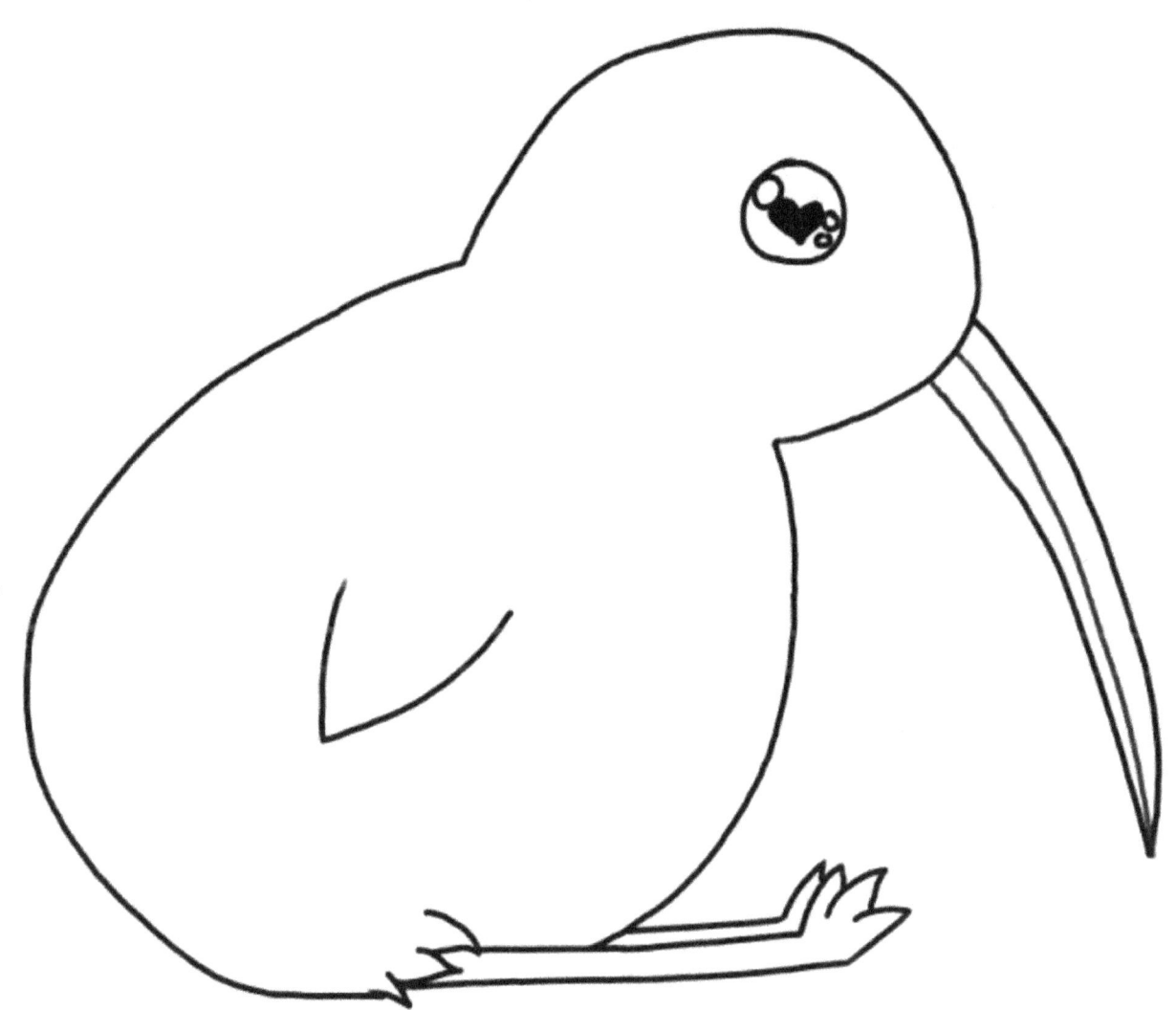

Name_____

Learning Takes Patience

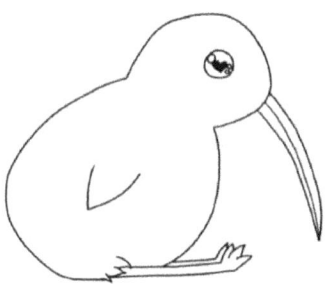 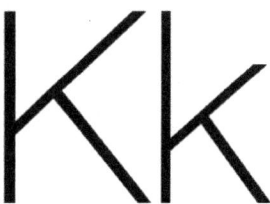

Ll
For Llama

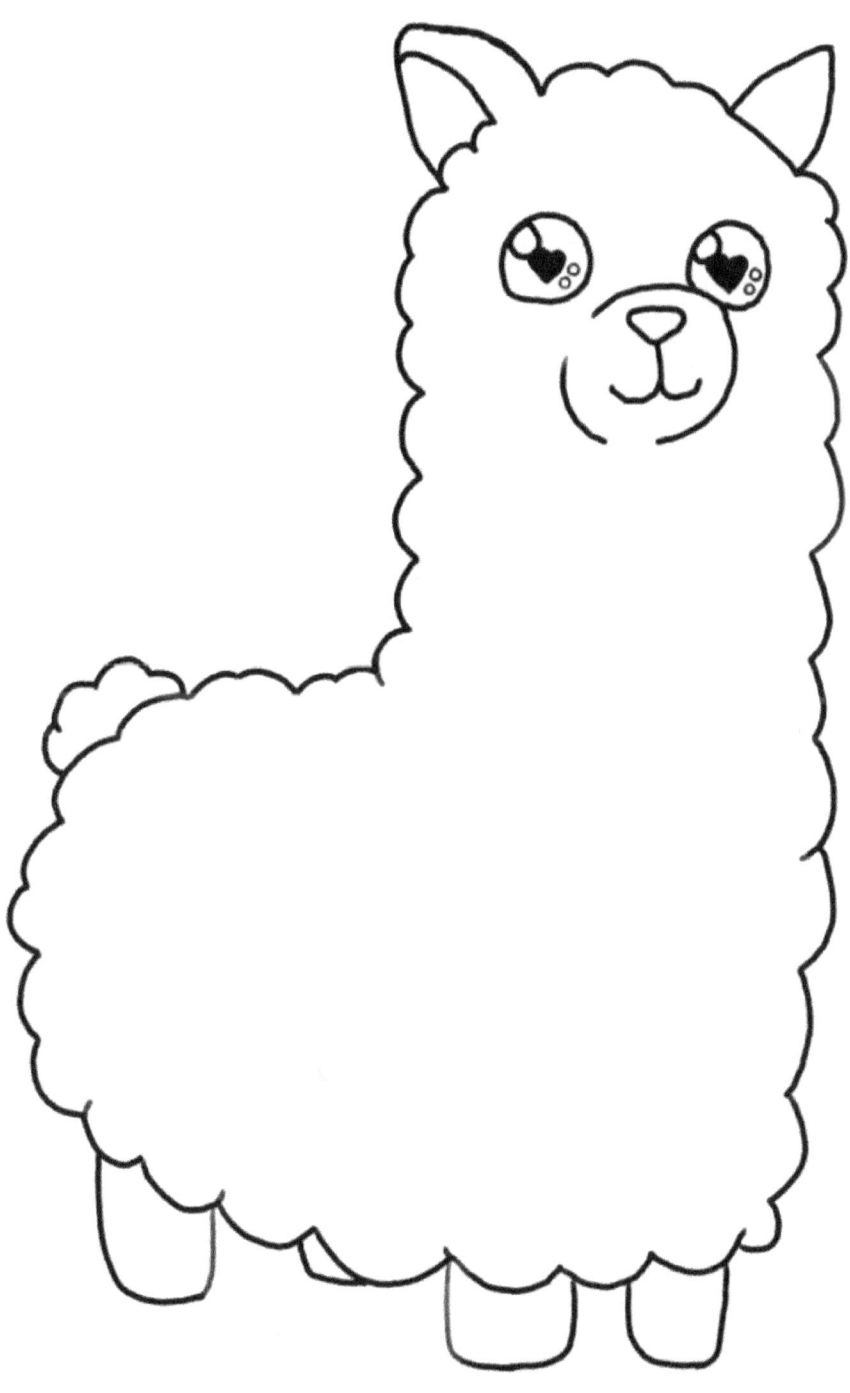

Name_____

Learning Takes Patience

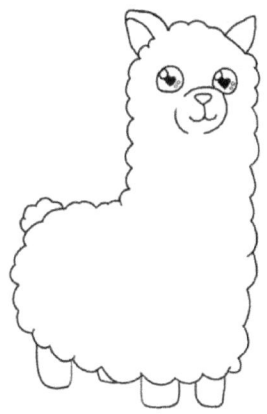

Ll

Mm
For Monkey

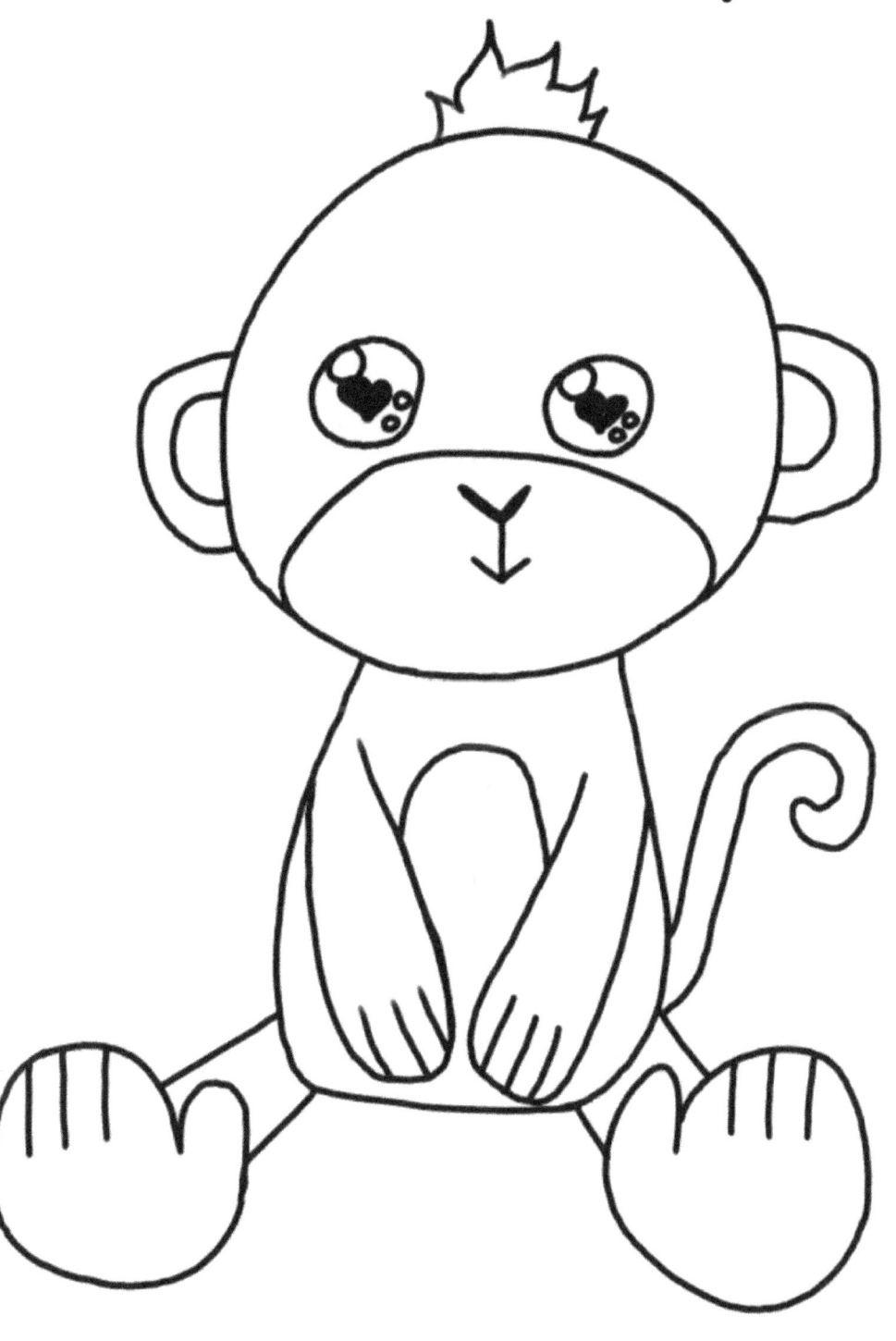

Name_____

Learning Takes Patience

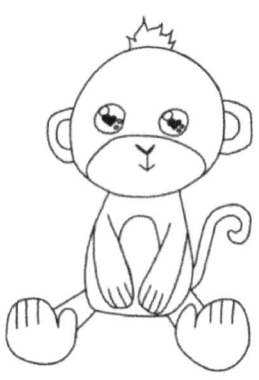

Mm

Nn
For Narwhal

Name_____

Learning Takes Patience

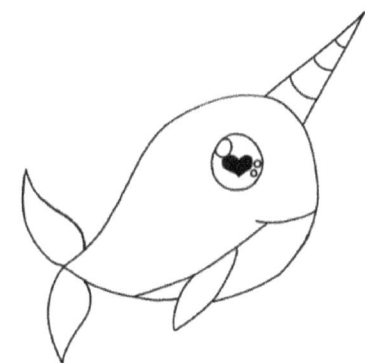

Nn

Oo
For Ocelot

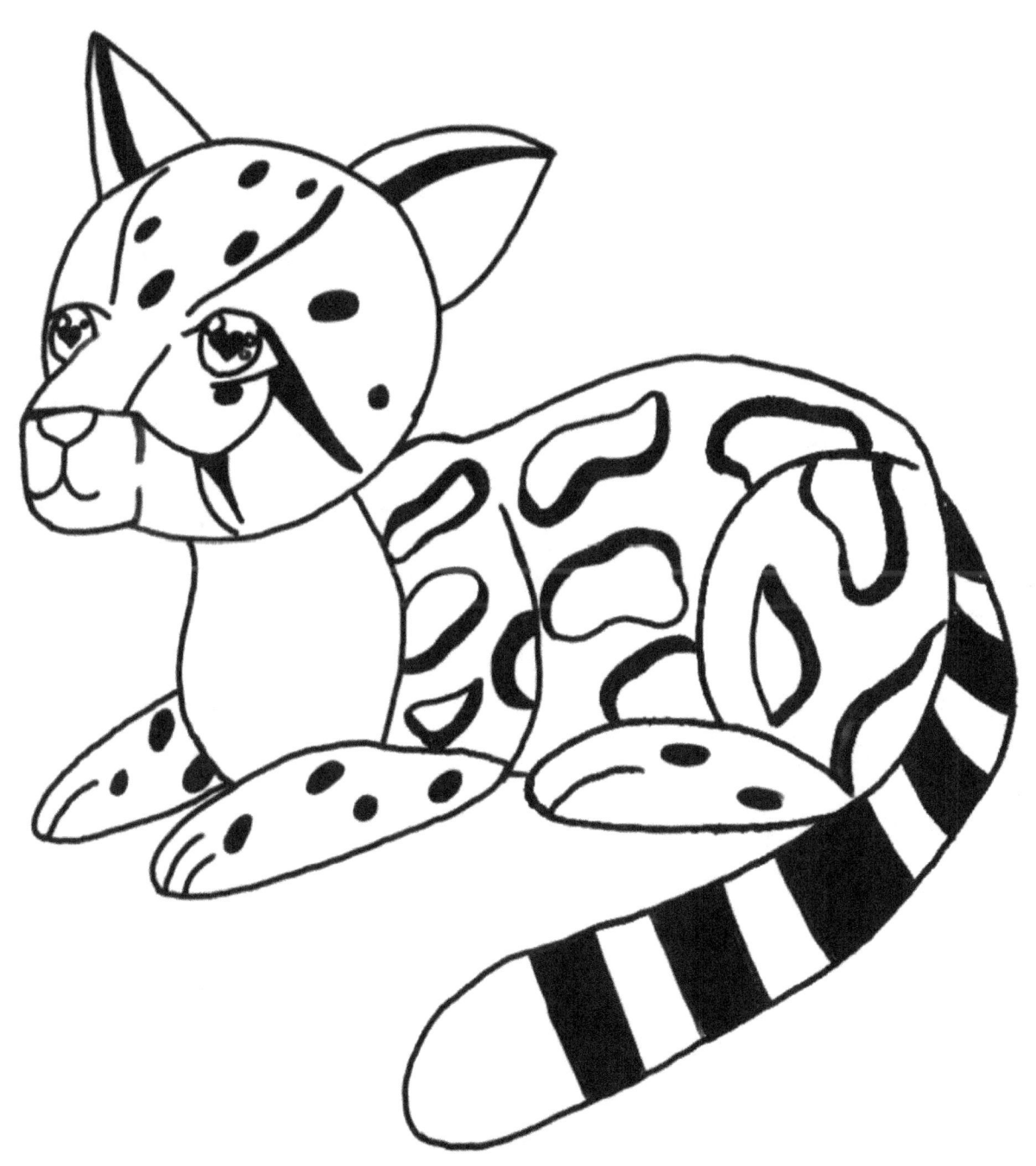

Name_____

Learning Takes Patience

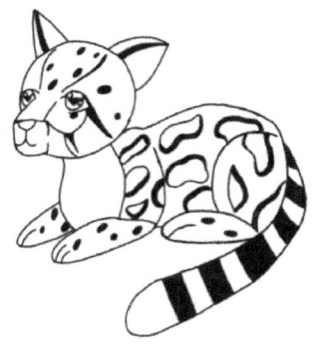
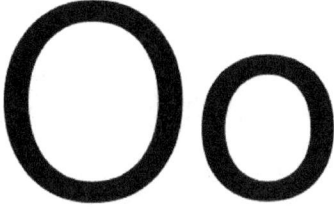

Pp
For Penguin

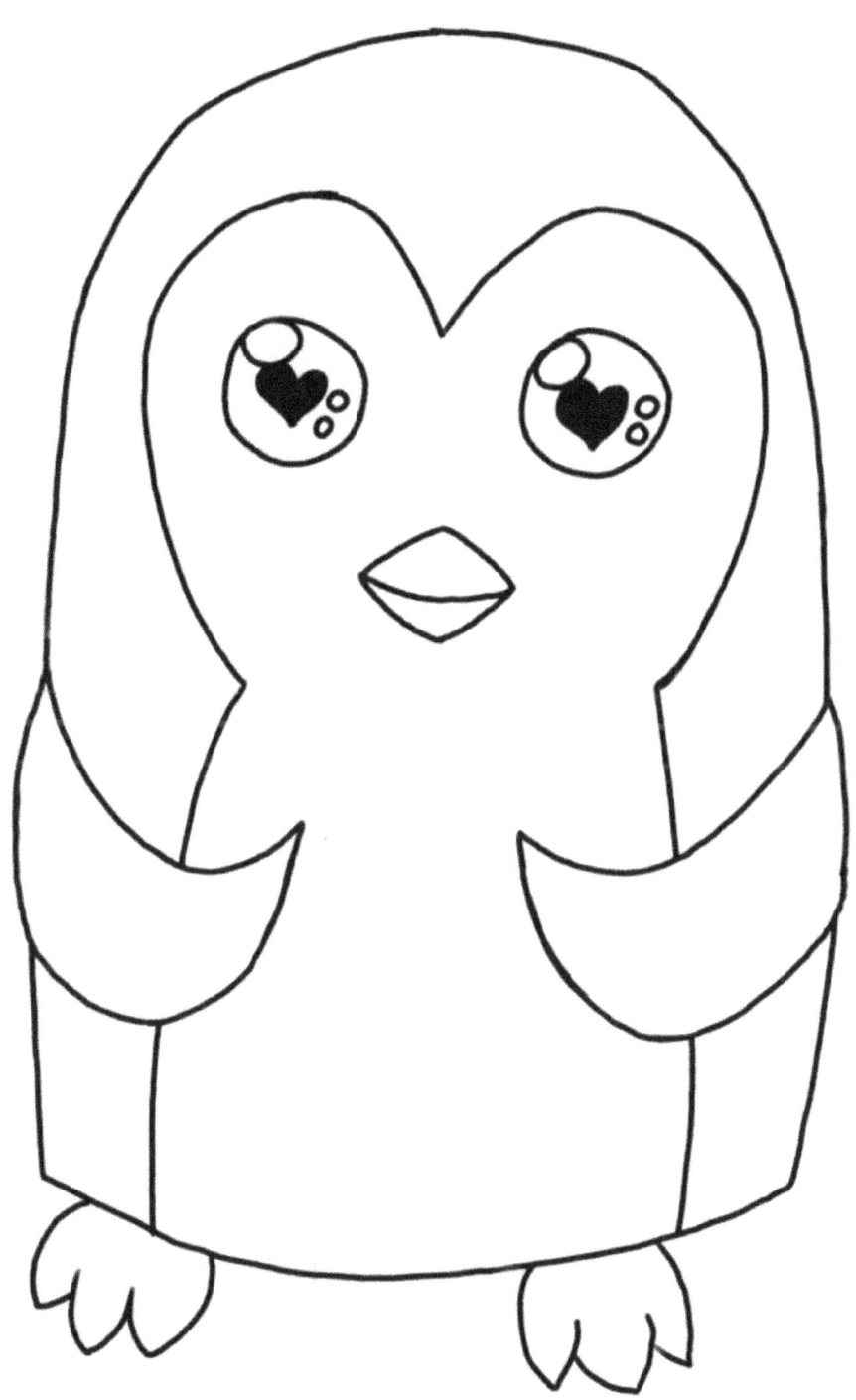

Name_____

Learning Takes Patience

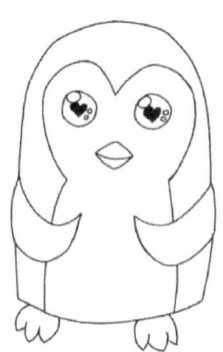

Pp

Qq
For Quoll

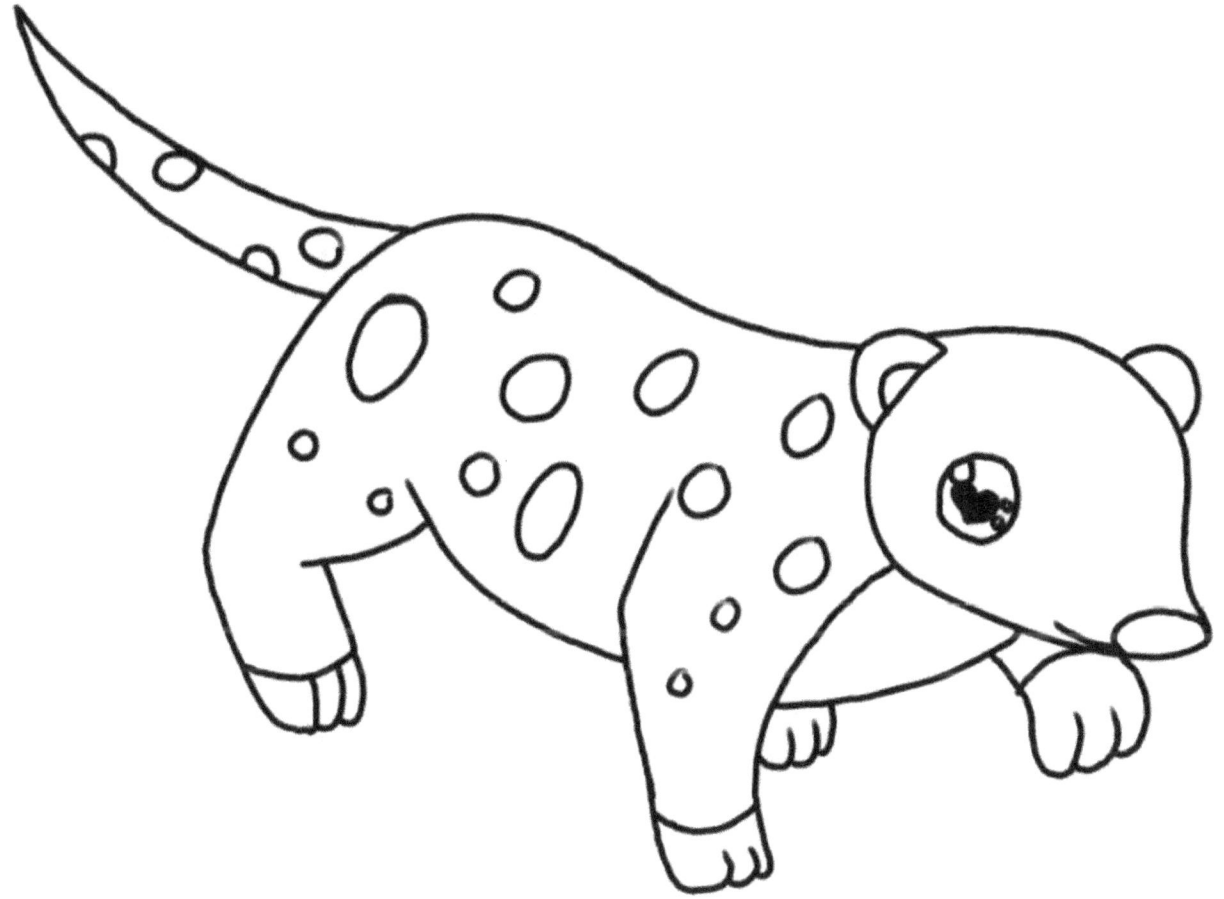

Name_____

Learning Takes Patience

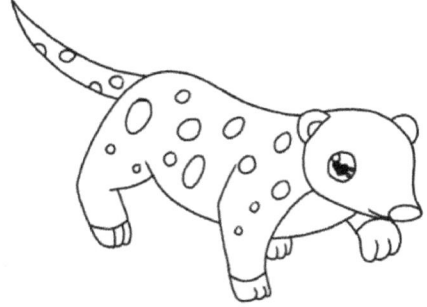

Qq

Rr
For Red Panda

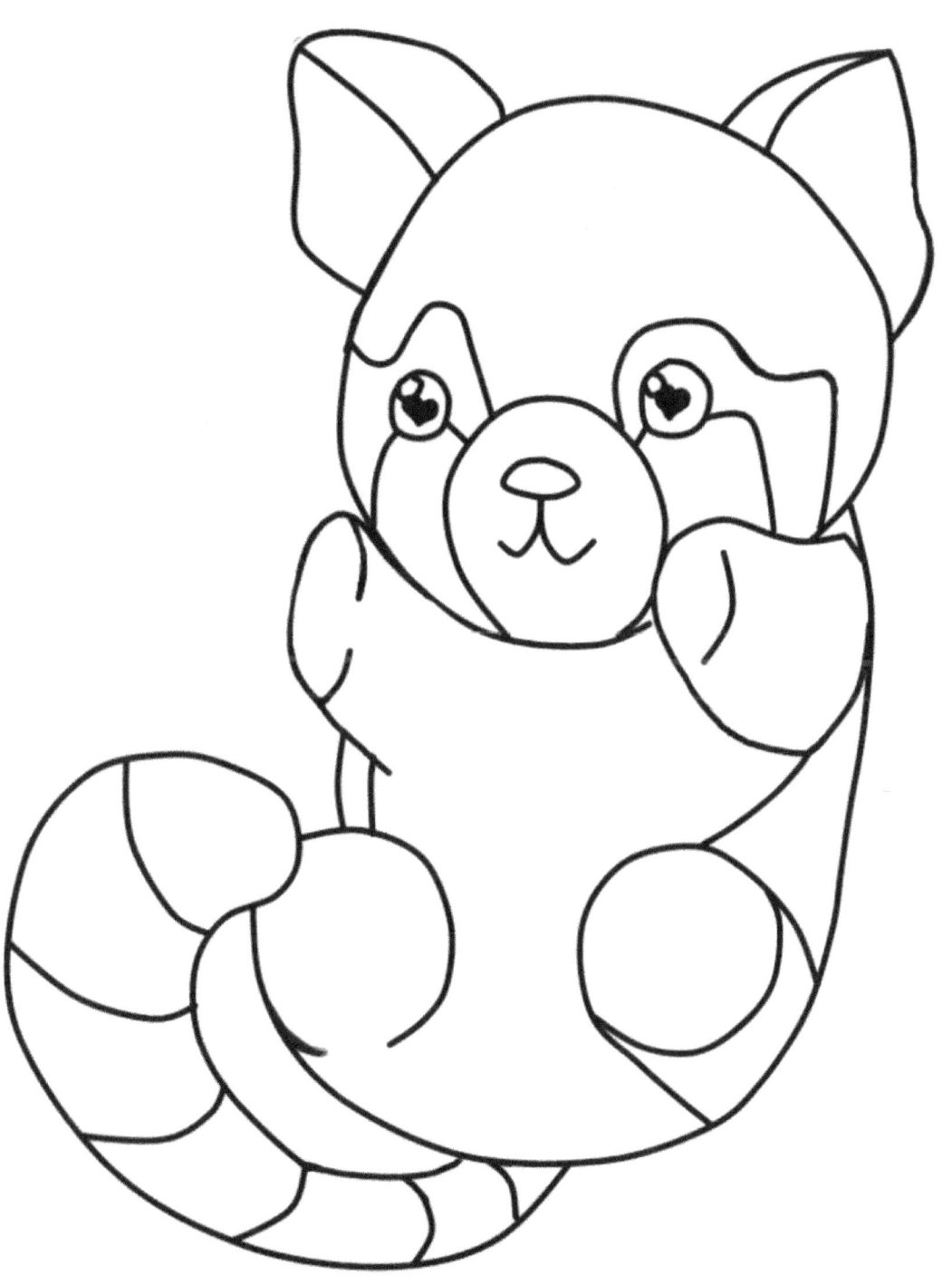

Name_____

Learning Takes Patience

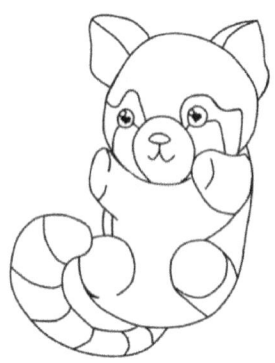

Rr

_____
- -
_____
- -
_____
- -
_____
- -
_____

Ss
For Salamander

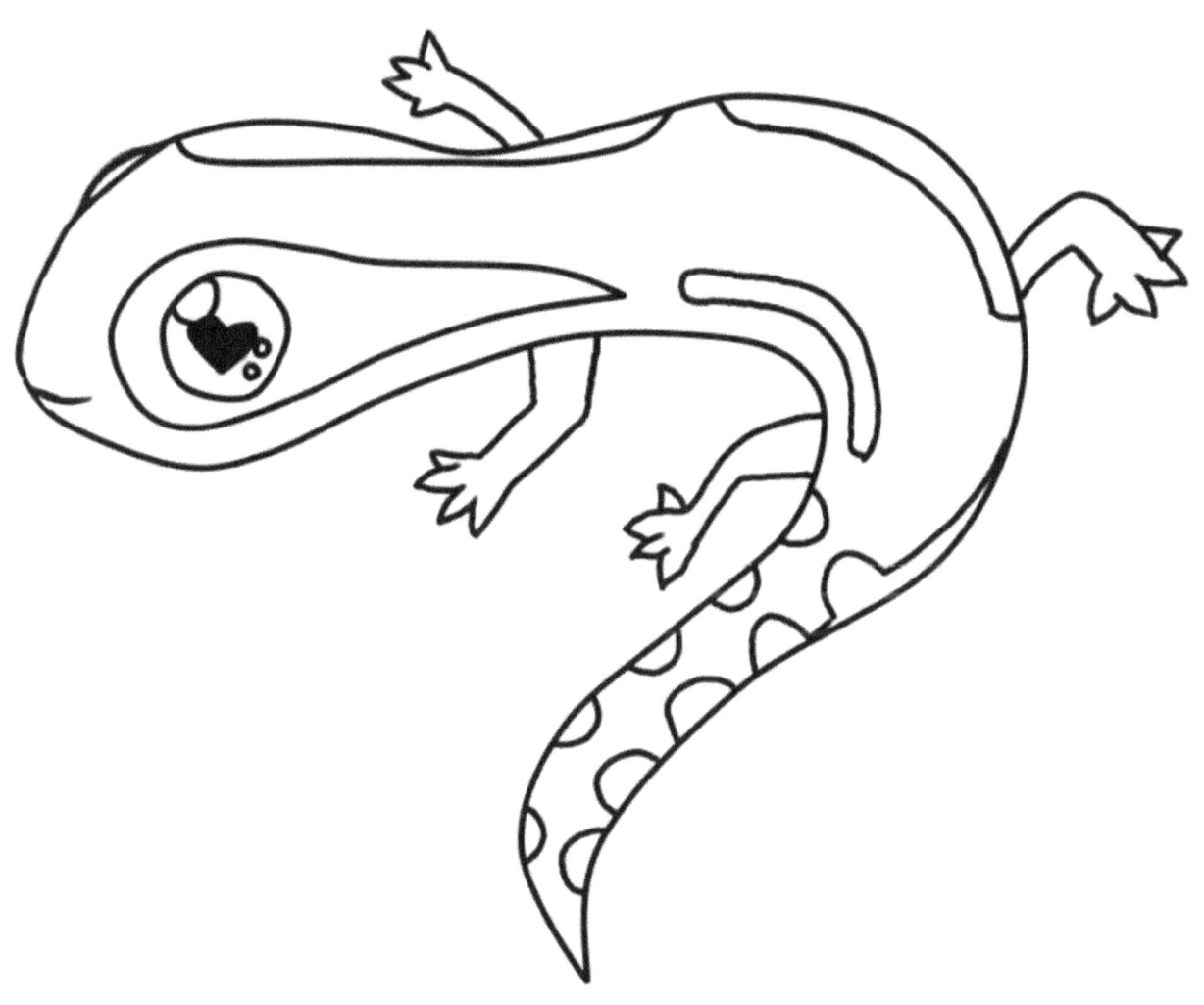

Name_____

Learning Takes Patience

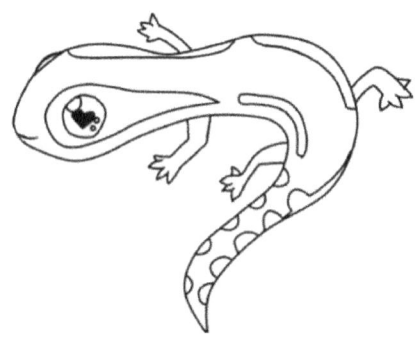

Ss

Tt
For Tadpole

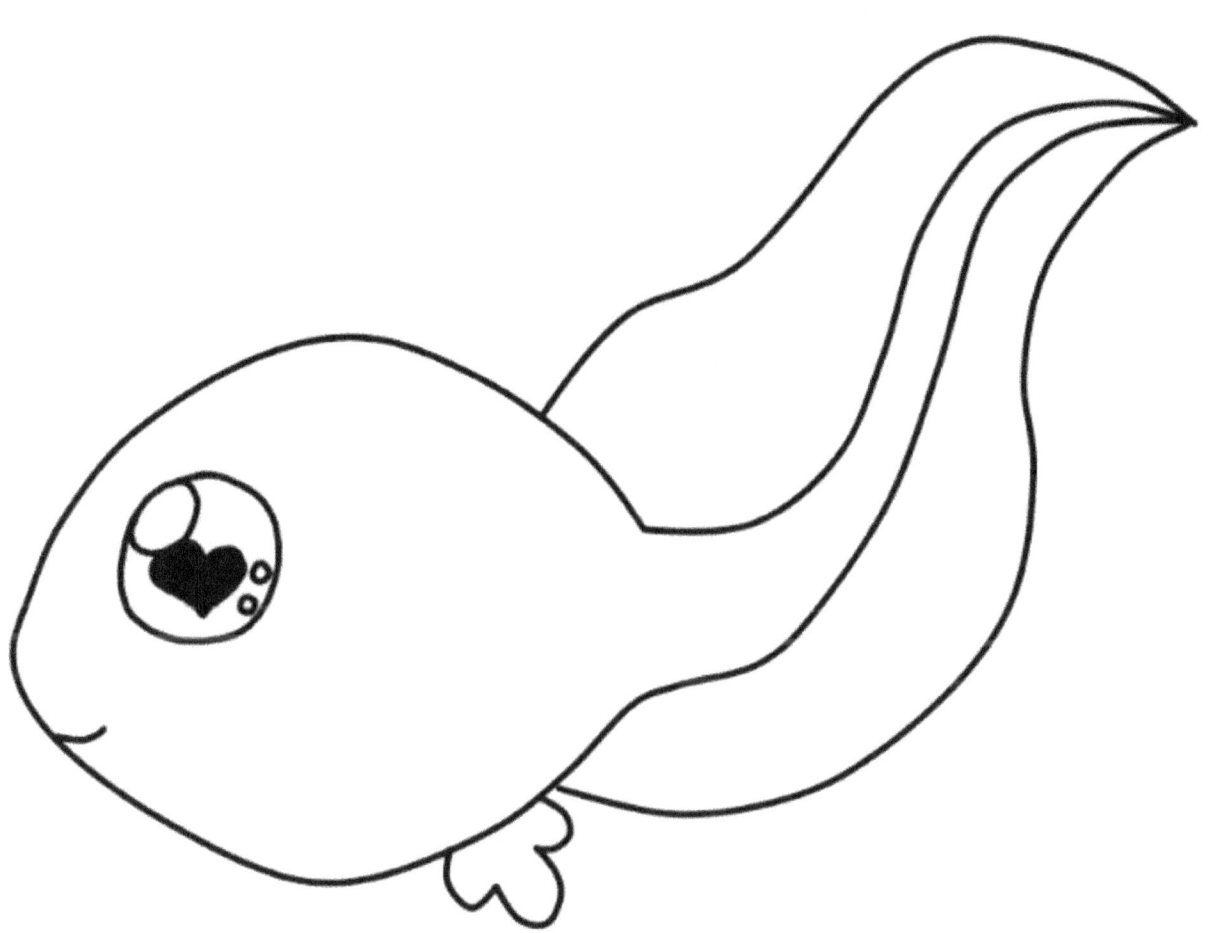

Name_____

Learning Takes Patience

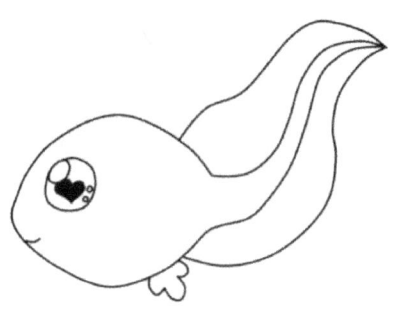

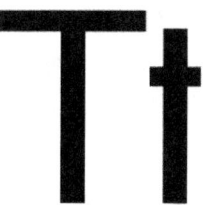

_____
- -
_____
- -
_____
- -
_____
- -
_____

Uu
For Unicorn

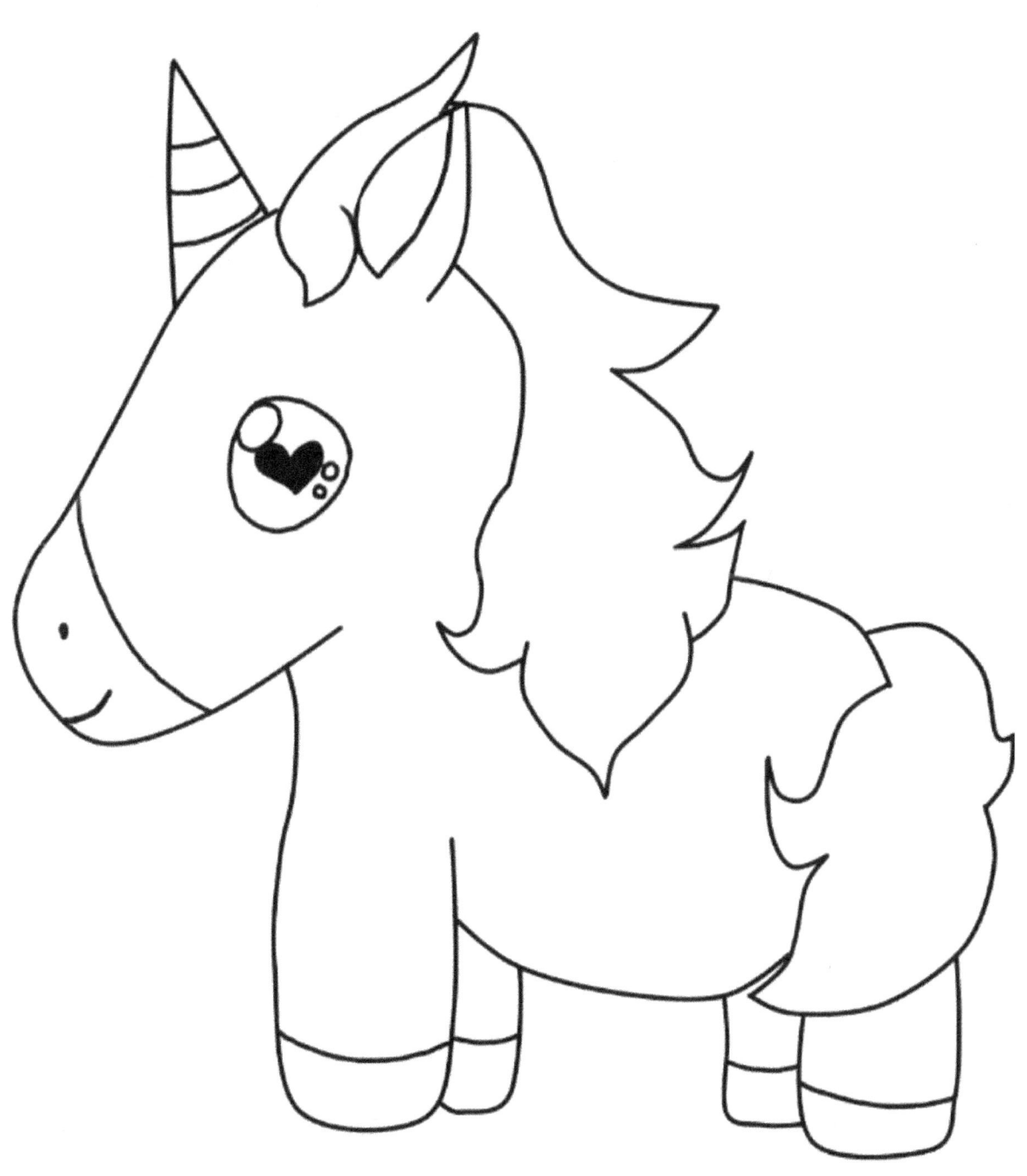

Name_____

Learning Takes Patience

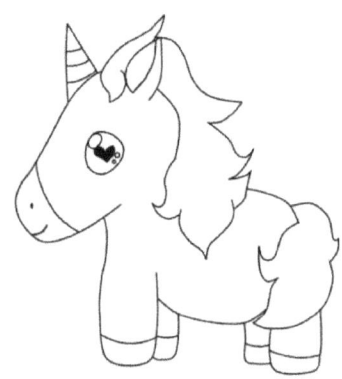

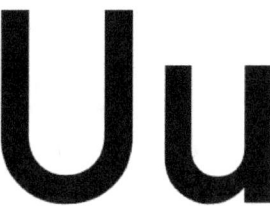

Vv
For Viper

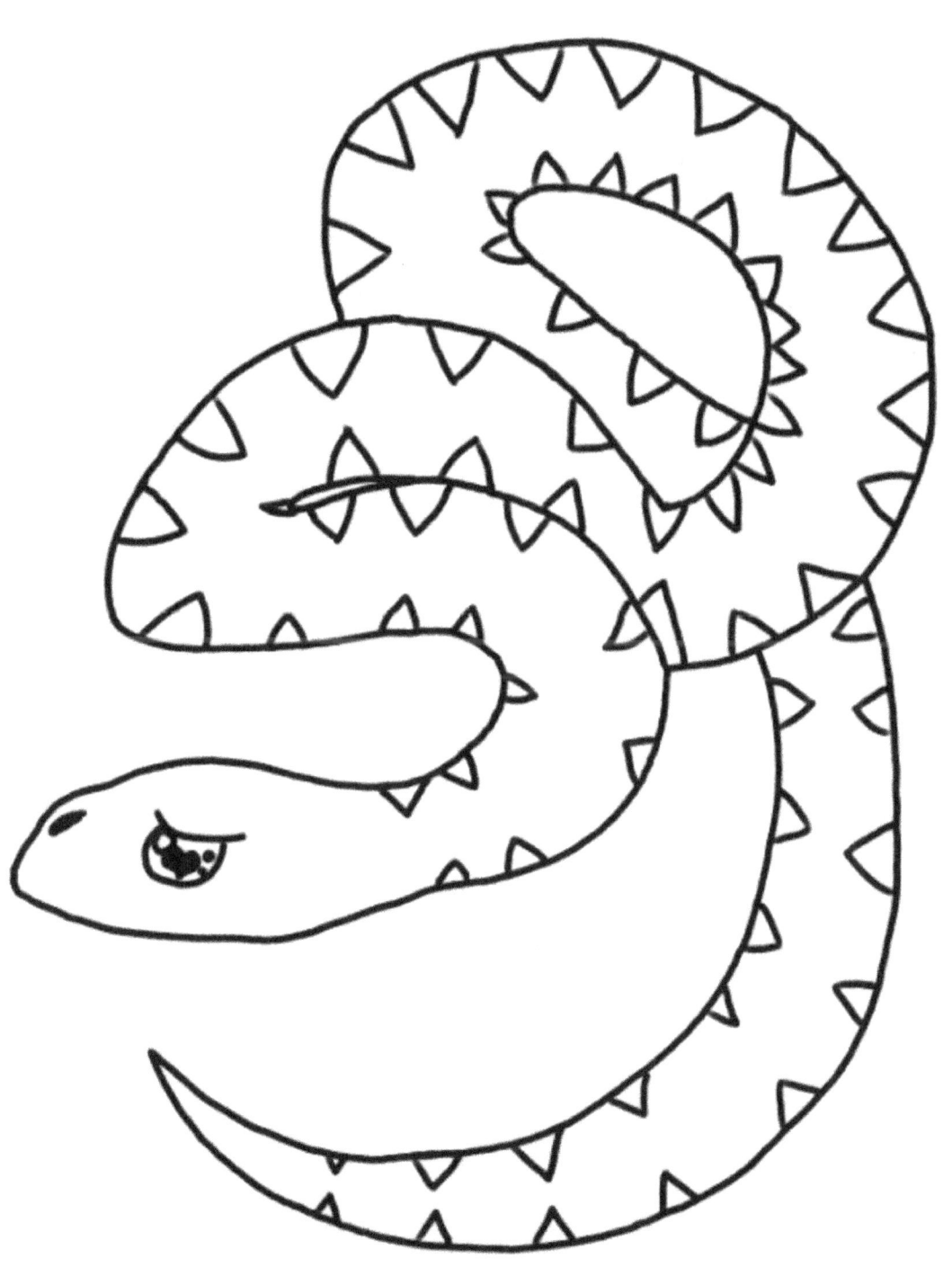

Name_____

Learning Takes Patience

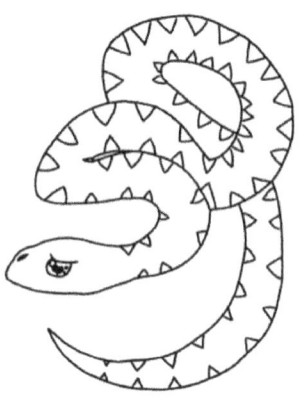

Vv

Ww
For Wolf

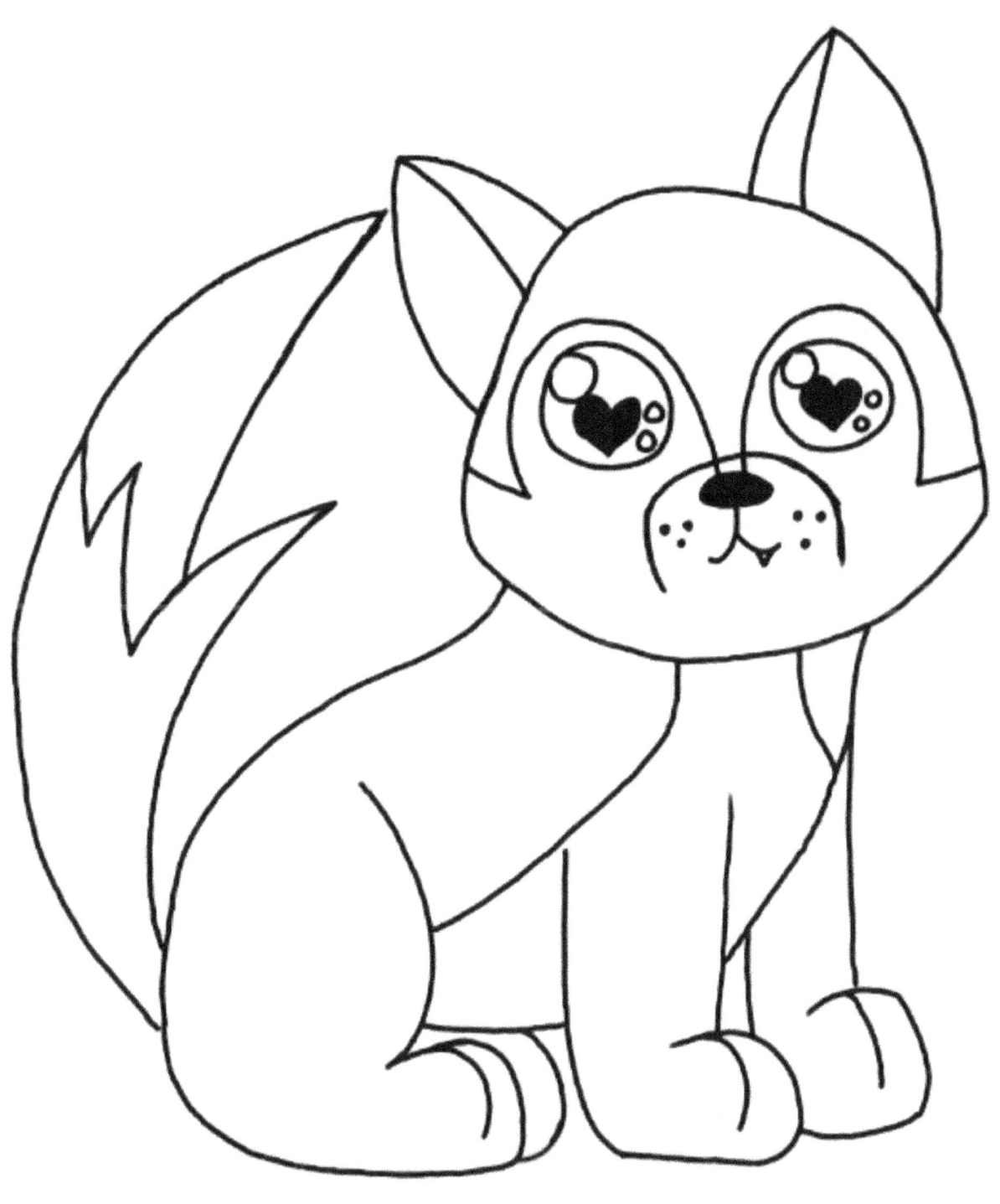

Name_____

Learning Takes Patience

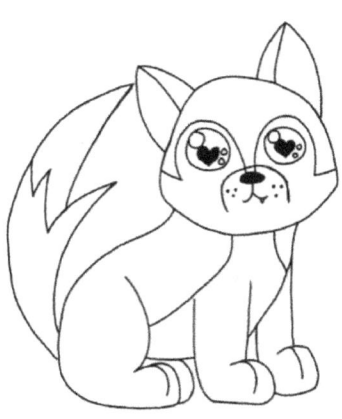

Ww

Xx
For X-Ray Fish

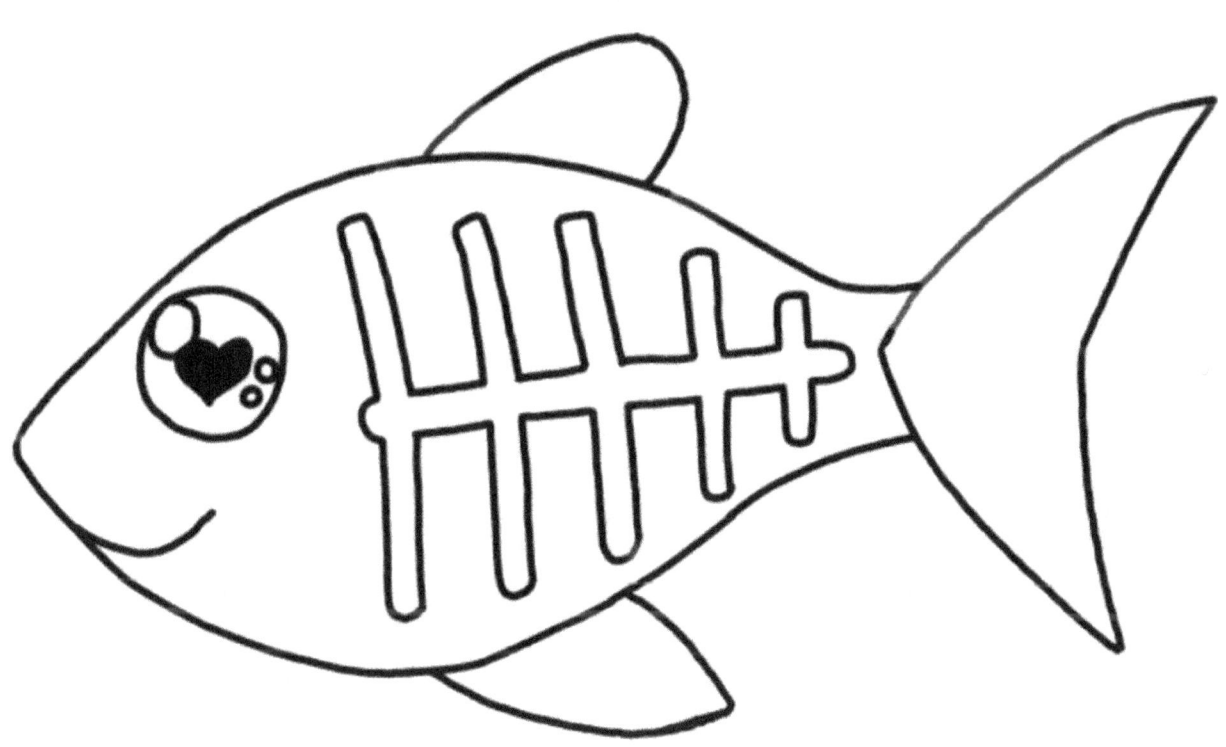

Name_____

Learning Takes Patience

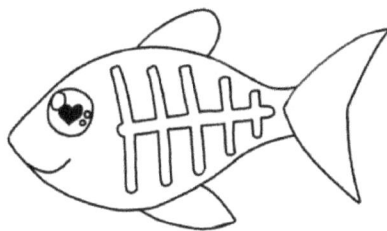

Xx

_____
- -
_____
- -
_____
- -
_____
- -

Yy
For Yabby

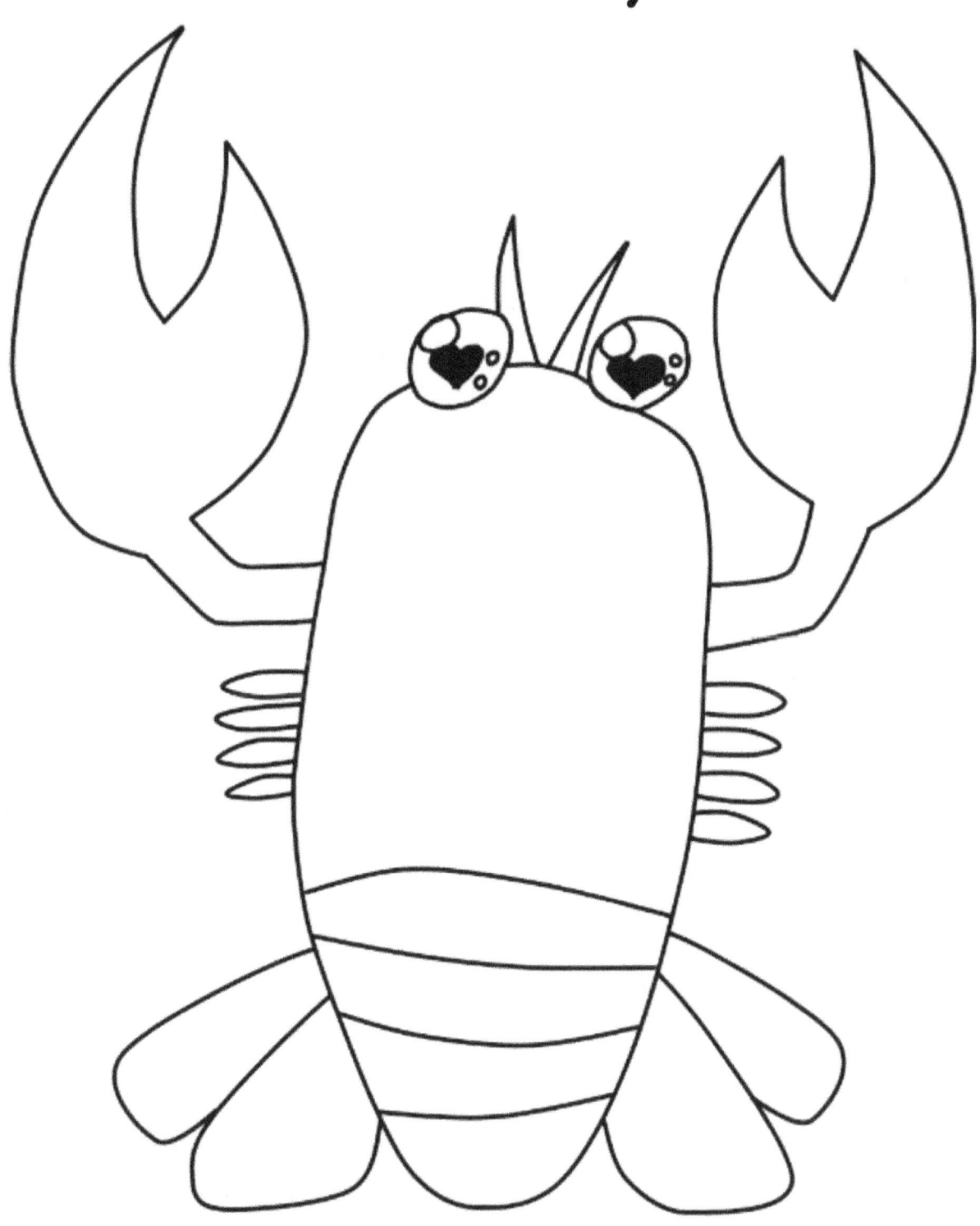

Name_____

Learning Takes Patience

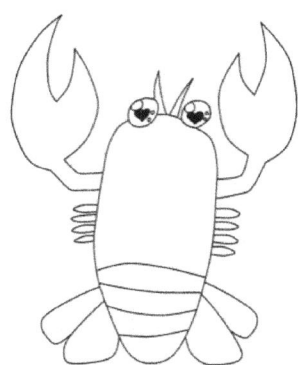

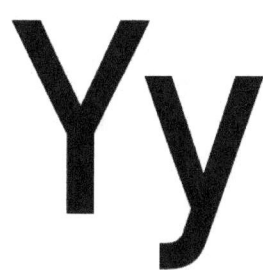

Zz
For Zebra

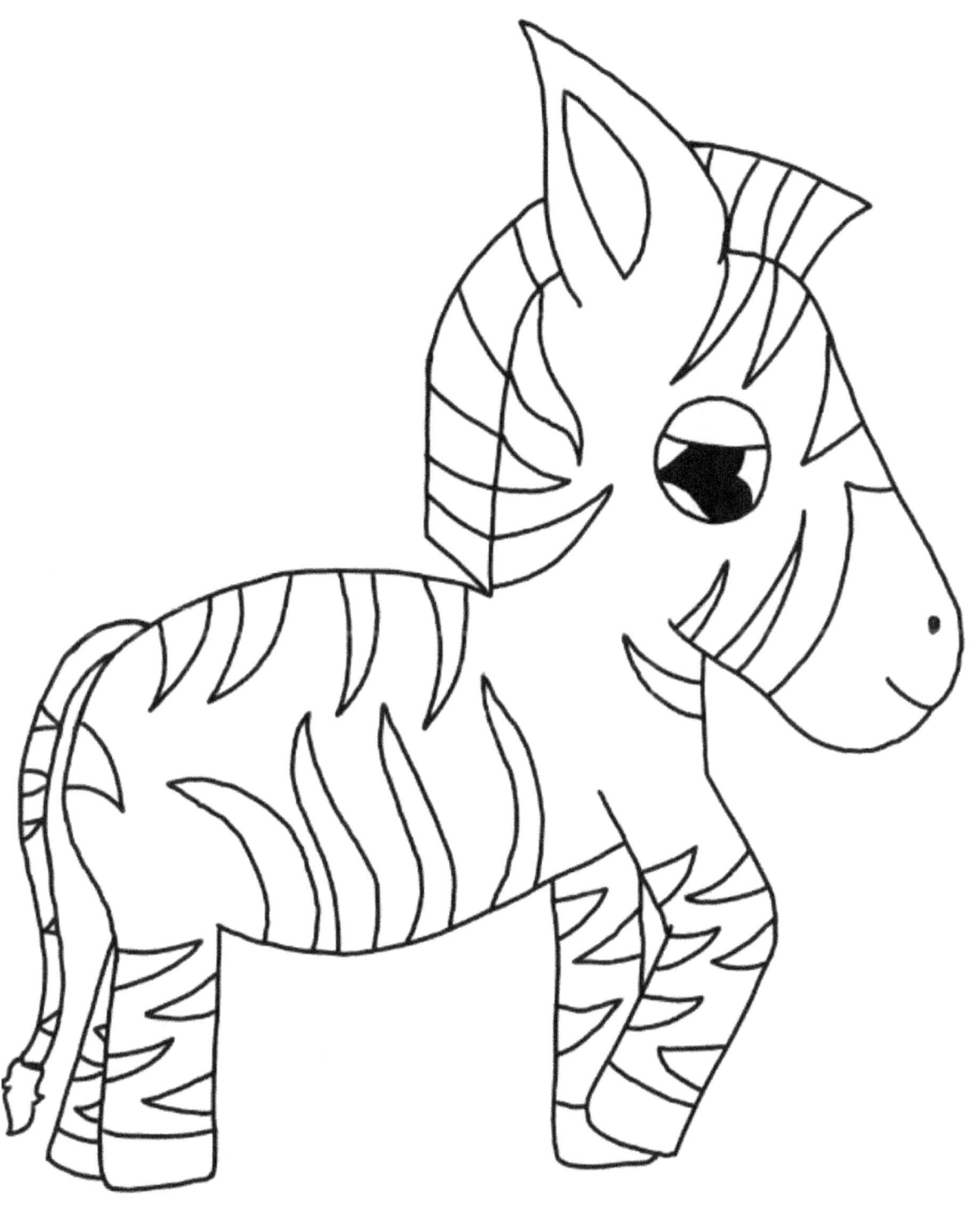

Name_____

Learning Takes Patience

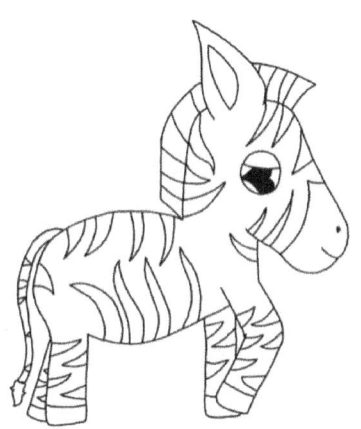

Zz

_____
- -
_____
- -
_____
- -
_____
- -
_____

www.ingramcontent.com/pod-product-compliance
Lightning Source LLC
Chambersburg PA
CBHW081441220526
45466CB00008B/2475